AMPERSANDS & ODDMENTS

AMPERSANDS & ODDMENTS

notes for a jobbing calligrapher

G. Roland Smith

 Skriber publications

AMPERSANDS & ODDMENTS

Notes for a Jobbing Calligrapher

Published by Skriber Publications
Collard House, School Lane, Hadlow
Tonbridge, Kent. TN11 0EH
01732 850 850

ISBN 978-0-9560885-0-5

British Library Cataloguing in Publication Data.
A catalogue record for this book is available from the British Library.

Set in 9pt. Garamond

Printed and bound in Great Britain by
L.E.A. Printers, 49 Leesons Hill, Orpington, Kent. BR5 2LF

ACKNOWLEDGEMENTS

I offer my warmest thanks to those good friends who have brought interesting ampersands to my notice, especially for the help of Gerald Bishop, Joan Bygrave, and John & Peter Cunningham. I gladly acknowledge the assistance of Dover Publications, MJB Typography and The Myriade Press. Mary Noble has also kindly allowed me to include her own lively selection, for which I am very grateful. Every attempt has been made to trace other examples which may still be in copyright: due restitution will be made in the case of any omissions.

In their attempts to outwit the computer, contemporary scribes, I am glad to say, have broken most of the rules. My interest in ampersands springs from the fact that here there are scarcely any rules to start with - almost any elegant little squiggle will do, and anyone may invent their own.

Lest this anarchic view of mine should offend the purists, however, let me say straight away that to form an expressive ampersand is by no means always easy, and to form one that relates to the script on either side can be distinctly tricky.

So I have assembled this little collection as a reference source to show some of the possibilities. But more than that - ampersands and other flourished signs and symbols are useful 'in their own right'. They provide the calligrapher with a demanding range of exercises which should be helpful in acquiring some fluency with the pen - they are fun to do, and rather beautiful when they are done well.

The old writing masters, for all their love of laying down the law, nevertheless displayed a certain daring and no-one could say they were not inventive. Their advice is maybe not as instructive today as it might have been in the 16th and 17th centuries, but there is still inspiration to be found if we look for it. I am inclined to think of them as exhibitionists rather than teachers and I wonder how practical they actually were: they have certainly influenced some of my examples here.

Just as printed letter-forms owed their origin to penscript - Gutenberg's Gothic is a prime example - so I have often reversed the process and turned to letterpress and lithographic founts in my search for interesting devices - they can frequently be re-interpreted with a calligraphic nib and lose nothing thereby.

Most of my examples have been written with some sort of metal nib - they are intended as 'script'. Also included, however, are a few 'drawn' examples constructed rather more laboriously. Illuminated ampersands are extremely rare since they never occur at the beginning of a sentence: they may, however, be appropriate, now and then, as part of a title: if not, who cares? The liberated scribe is free to exploit letter-forms for their own sake - for their visual effect.

It is perhaps a little strange that so short a word as 'and' or 'et' should ever have been in need of abbreviation at all. I suspect that the ampersand did not come about in order to save space: it probably just happened with the passage of time because, being short, and being frequently used, it simply evolved into the 'shorthand' symbol we now know. Nevertheless, it is an abbreviation, and as such has got many a scribe out of a tight corner.

As a linking device, rather than just another word, the ampersand can also serve to tie things together more dramatically. The initials of bride and groom on a wedding invitation, if they do not lend themselves to a monogram, can at least be united with the careful lovers' knot of a flourished ampersand.

Frederic Goudy was a prolific American typographer of great distinction working in the first half of the twentieth century. His designs were for metal type, but being well-versed in the calligraphic styles of earlier times, he often sought to retain their essential spirit, whilst adapting their forms to meet the demands of the founders and in the interest of legibility. The influence of the quill may be clearly seen in many of these examples.

Goudy himself said in his autobiography: 'In 1936 I was honored by a request of the Typophiles to contribute something to its volume in preparation on Ampersands. I had been making ampersands for my types for years without giving much thought to their origin, except that for the greater number of them I endeavored to convey the idea of "et" in each. Beyond that point they hadn't particularly interested me, until one day when my friend Howard Coggeshall, the printer of Utica, asked me what I was doing and I said "I was drawing some ampersands." After about half-an-hour's cogitation he came back with "What the H- is an ampersand" - and I told him. When he had gone I said to myself that if a printer like Howard didn't know what an ampersand was, there must be many writers, typographers, advertisers, etc., who don't know either. So I looked in the dictionary and encyclopedia and found, except for a few lines in each that the matter was almost a secret, so I began looking into it. Of course all this is beside the purposes of the present volume, but as my research led to the drawing and engraving of *sixty-five* ampersands to illustrate my contribution to the Typophile book, I feel that a mention and showing of a few of them here may not be out of place, since they are a part of my type-founding output.'

Designs by Frederic W Goudy prepared in 1936 for *The Typophiles*, and included in his autobiography first published in 1946 entitled *A Half-Century of Type Design and Typography, 1895-1945'* and re-issued in 1978 by The Myriade Press. *With acknowledgement to The Myriade Press, New Rochelle.*

An assortment of printers' display type as shown in a 20th.century typesetters' advertisement. Note how several of these are clearly calligraphic in origin.

With acknowledgement to mjb typography, New York.

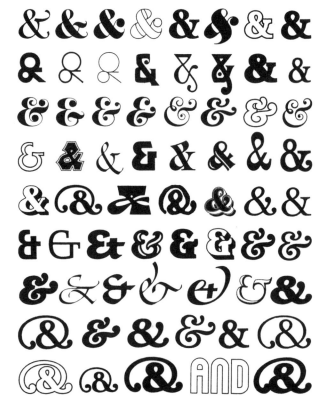

A selection of 'drawn' examples - highly specialised and invented for that one-off occasion, or for no occasion at all, these designs have broken the boundaries of conventional usage, and can scarcely be regarded any more as letter-forms. But you never know, that special book cover or poster could allow the scribe to indulge their imagination. Notice that these curiosities suggest their own sphere - ecclesiastical, mechanical, musical, horticultural, architectural, historical and so on.

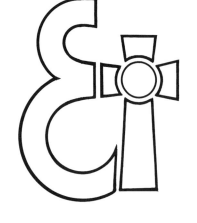

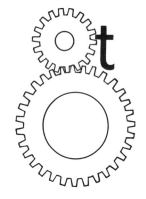

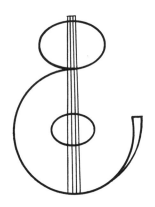

The ampersand is said to be derived from the Latin word for 'and' - *'et'* . These two letters have undoubtedly influenced most forms of ampersand and they can still be recognised in some current examples. The Romans, however, also had their own shorthand marks for everyday use - these would be necessary when taking down messages at speed when the only means of recording speech was by handwriting. Their sign for *'et'* was rather like our figure '7'.

Confessio ꞇ pulcrntudo in conspectu eius: sanctimonia ꞇ magnificencia

The Luttrell Psalter, c.1340, famous for its marginal scenes of everyday rural life in the 14th.century, is written throughout in a consistently magnificent Gothic style in which many ampersands of this sort are to be found.

A passage from the first printed Latin psalter produced in Mainz in 1457. Although issued under the imprint of Johannes Fust and Peter Schöffer, the book owes its existence to the technology perfected by their erstwhile partner Gutenberg. In his efforts to reproduce all the subtlety of hand-written Gothic script, Gutenberg was by no means content with just the simple letters of the alphabet, but cast also hundreds of typographic abbreviations and clusters of joined letters. Several of these can be found in this extract from the first psalm as, for example, in *'die ac nocte'* (day and night) where the 'c' and 't' are cleverly fused. Note also the other form of 'and' - *'et'*. The larger versal capitals were probably hand-painted in red.

lūtas ei⁹: et in lege eius meditabit die ac nocte, Et erit tanḡ lignū qd plātatū ist secus deciursus aꝗē: qd fructū suū dabit in tꝑe suo Et foliū ei⁹ nō defluet: ⁊ oīa ꝗcūꝗ faciet ꝓsperabūt, Nō sic impij nō sic sed tanḡ pului quē ꝓicit ventus a facie terre,

A passage from *'Recuyell of the Histories of Troye'* printed by William Caxton around 1476. Caxton introduced printing to England: he was himself author, translator, publisher and printer. His English prose, despite its curious spelling - he presumably made his own rules - is still readable today. Although only about twenty years after Gutenberg, Caxton's type style is certainly different, still clearly derived from a pen-script, it has a more rounded 'homespun' look. Notice that when a lower-case 'd' falls at the end of a word it is closely followed by a descending hook: this already gives the word *'and'* a rather distinctive appearance which could possibly have influenced the evolution of the ampersand.

In these two bokes precedentr. we haue by the helpe of god, tretyd, of the two first destructyons of Troye with the noble fiytes and, dedes of the stronge and, puissant Hercules .that made and, dyde so many mervayllis that the engyne humayn of alle men oughte to meruaylle. And, also how he slewe the kynge Laomedon dete doun and, put his cyte of troye to rupne Now in the thirde and, laste boo k god, to fore . we shall saie how the sayd, cyte was by Priamus sone of the said, kynge laomedon rediffied and repayred moze stronge and, moze pupssante than euer hit was before . And, afterward, how for the rauysssement of dame Helayne wyf of kynge Menelaus of grece . the sayd, cyte was totally destroyed, Priamus hector and, alle his sones slayn with noblesse wyth out nombre . as hit shall app ere in the proces of the chapitres ..

15

These examples are from the Book of Kells, one of the most famous of all early 'Celtic' treasures. Similar letter-forms are found in the Book of Durrow, the Lindisfarne Gospels, the Lichfield Gospels and other notable manuscripts. Celtic designs, even after fifteen centuries or so, still faintly resonate with the mystical symbolism that, no doubt, went into their making. Fanciful creatures are to be found in their pages, and the intricacy of their decoration suggests a love of riddles or magical formulae. Celtic style jewellery and fabrics are popular today because they bring a welcome touch of fantasy into our lives. The comfortable rounded shapes belong with the generous 'uncial' text, whereas the straight-line version is found on the elaborately ornate title-pages.

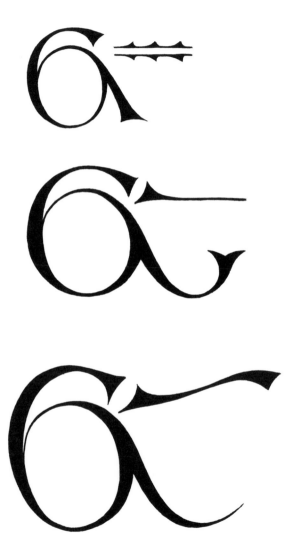

cipes sacerdotum &ingressus inatrio
sedebat cum ministris ut uideret pñe
rei. **P**rincipes autem sacerdotum &
omne conalium querebant falsum
testimonium contra ihin uteum morta
traderent &non inuenerunt cum &cum
multa falsi testes accesserent. Nouissi
me autem uenerunt duo falsi testes &

Part of the *Lichfield Gospels*
with ampersands in evidence

vigilate & orate

Urbi & Orbi

St George & the Dragon

Trade & Industry

18

Ebb & Flow

Tripe & Onions

FIT & WELL

Soft & Low

Bell, book & candle

Down & Out

David &c Goliath

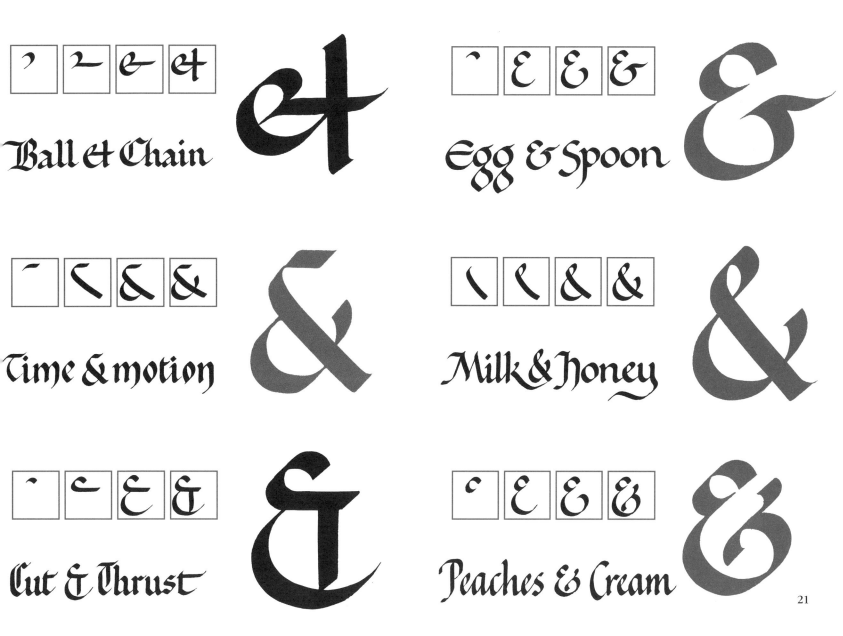

Ball & Chain

Egg & Spoon

Time & motion

Milk & Honey

Cut & Thrust

Peaches & Cream

21

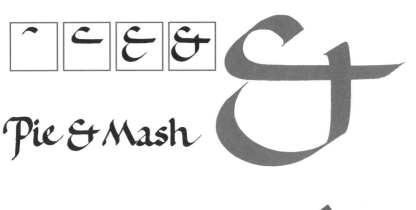

Pie & Mash

Time & Again

There & Then

Vide et Crede

Pepper & salt

Rose & Crown

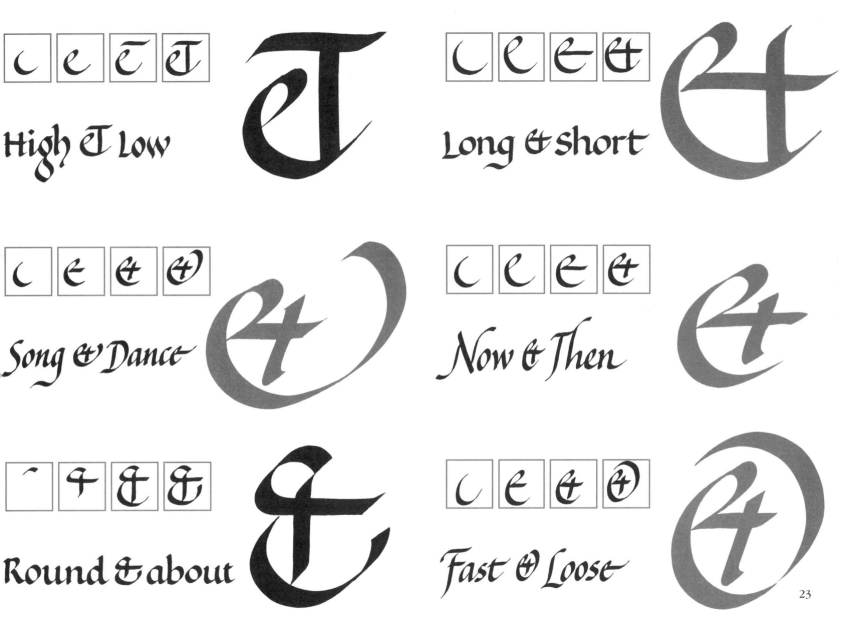

High & Low

Long & short

Song & Dance

Now & Then

Round & about

Fast & Loose

23

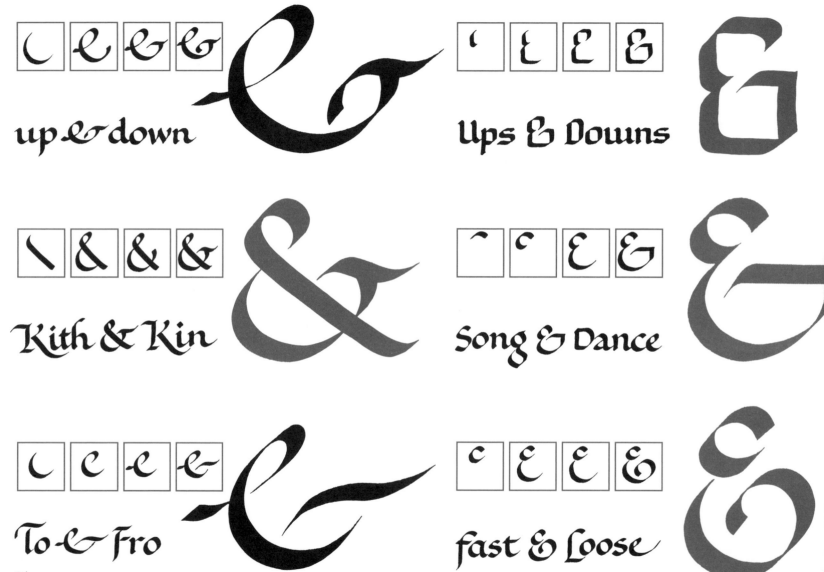

up & down

Ups & Douns

Kith & Kin

Song & Dance

To & Fro

fast & Loose

24

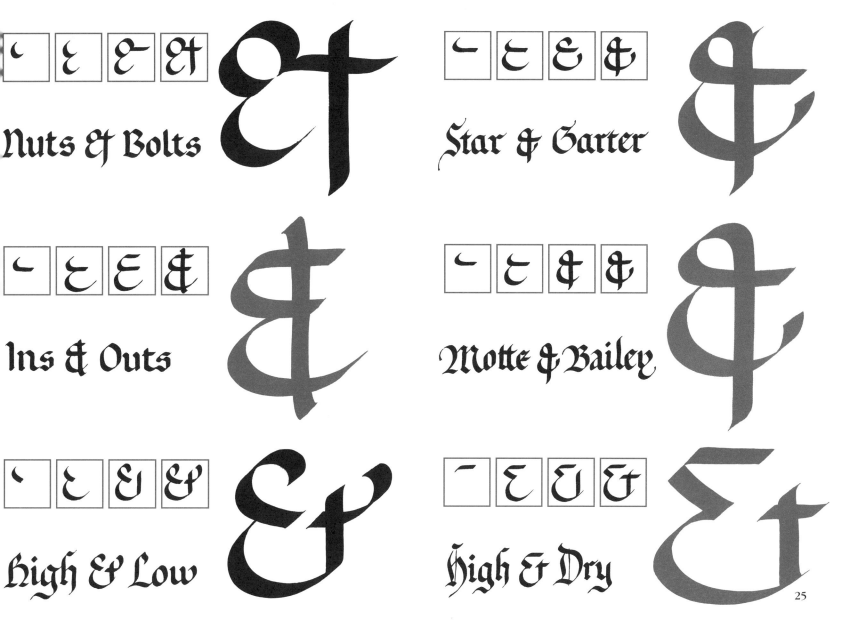

Nuts & Bolts

Star & Garter

Ins & Outs

Motte & Bailey

High & Low

High & Dry

Back & Forth

Time & Tide

Pen & Ink

Fine & Dandy

Cat & Mouse

Home & Dry

Oddities

There is now a wealth of scholarly material dealing with the minutiae of scribal activity over the centuries. The ordinary jobbing calligrapher, however, will scarcely be much concerned with these historical niceties, any more than were his antecedents.

We have here a few odd-looking devices which the experts have identified from different periods - dates approximate. If you can still make out the letters 'et' it's a ligature; if not, it's an ampersand.

The slightly ungainly 'at' sign has achieved notoriety with the advent of the computer. On some occasions now the calligrapher may be required to set down an 'e-mail' address, for example, and may find the @ rather tricky. I find it best to inscribe the 'a' first and then add the outer pen-strokes.

| Uncial 8th.c. | Half-Uncial 9th.c. | Insular 9th.c. | Gothic 12th.c. | French 14th.c. | Batarde 15th.c. | Rotunda 15th.c. |

With the refinement of printing from movable type in the mid 15th.century the rôle of the scribe was bound to change dramatically. No longer did he need to slave away year after year inscribing weighty tomes, but he was certainly not made redundant. This great leap in information technology happened to coincide with a period of expansion in trade and exploration: the settlement of new lands, the exchange of goods, the allocation of property and a rise in scholarly activity gave cause for legal transactions of one sort and another. Only a few copies of such legal documents would be required - not sufficient to warrant the laborious setting up of metal type. They did, however, call for some degree of literacy among the merchant classes and in court circles.

So there evolved a new breed of scribes - the 'writing masters' - experts with the pen, who offered advice to the uninitiated in the form of writing manuals - short books of instruction which could fairly easily be run off in limited editions on the new printing presses. They nearly all exhibit an amazing virtuosity with the pen or quill, and a dexterity which surely few could ever hope to emulate. They were printed from wood blocks - or, later on, from metal plates, the engraving of which was a wonderful skill in itself. The scribes did not always do their own engraving. Despite their showmanship, the writing masters did, in the long run, influence subsequent writing styles. Their love of ampersands is apparent in the following examples.

From a writing manual by Lesgret of Paris, 1694

Le Livre d'Exemplaires

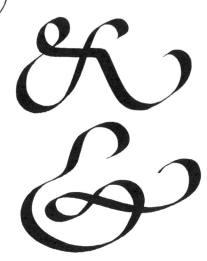

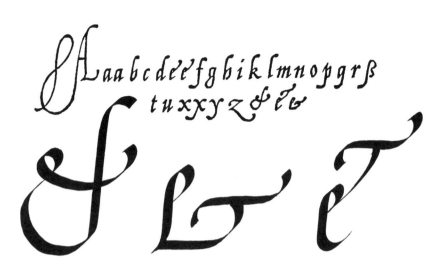

From a writing manual by Palatino of Rome, 1548

Libro, nel qual s'Insegna a Scrivere

Demostene Interrogato a che modo nell' Arte del dire fusse piu Eccell.te degli altri, rispose, consumando piu olio che Vino. Pitagora, diceua l'Arte: senza la esercitatione niente essere, et la esercitatione senza l'arte esser esser nulla. &c.

From a writing manual by Boissens of Amsterdam, 1594
Promtuarium and below a rather scratchy alphabet by
Hamon of Lyon, 1580
Alphabet de l'Invention des Lettres

.a.b.c.d.e.f.g.h.i.k.l.m.n.o.p.q.r.ʃ.s.t.v.u.x.y.z.&.

Another example from *A Tutor to Penmanship* by Ayres of London, c.1698. Note the strong verticality and very close letter-spacing.

Two decisive English examples - above by Ayre of London, c.1698
from *A Tutor to Penmanship*
and below from *Practical Penmanship* by Richard Clark,
also of London, 1758

From a writing manual published in 1540 by the Dutch cartographer and mathematician Gerardus Mercator (1512-1594).

The alphabet resembles those eloquent and expressive italic styles that originated in Italy. Notice that the flourishes spring naturally from the letter-forms themselves and show no sign of having been subsequently attached.

An assortment of rather quirky
flamboyant ampersands - maybe
useful in connection with the
more cursive forms of italic
- but not for the faint-hearted.

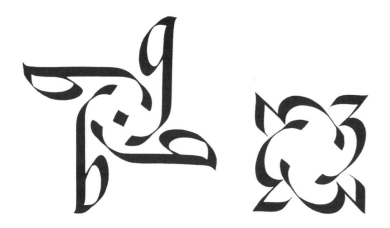

These devices serve no grammatical purpose but can sometimes be used decoratively with text to good effect. On their own, they make intriguing patterns for greetings cards and suchlike.

They also offer a fairly painless means of practising letter-forms in a purely visual way, judging angles and distances. They are made by taking a letter - or group of letters - and rotating the paper through ninety degrees between every repetition. Letters with ascenders or descenders are particularly useful to play with. If lacking in confidence, the scribe may prefer to plot the composition in advance with the help of tracing paper or squared graph paper.

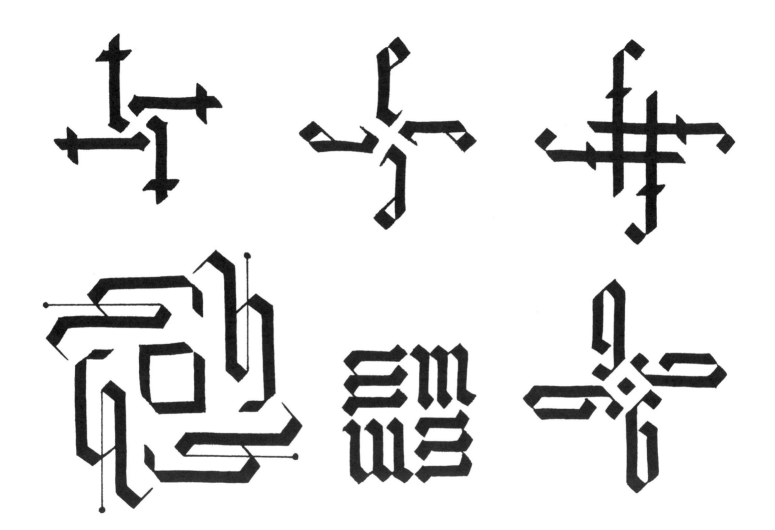

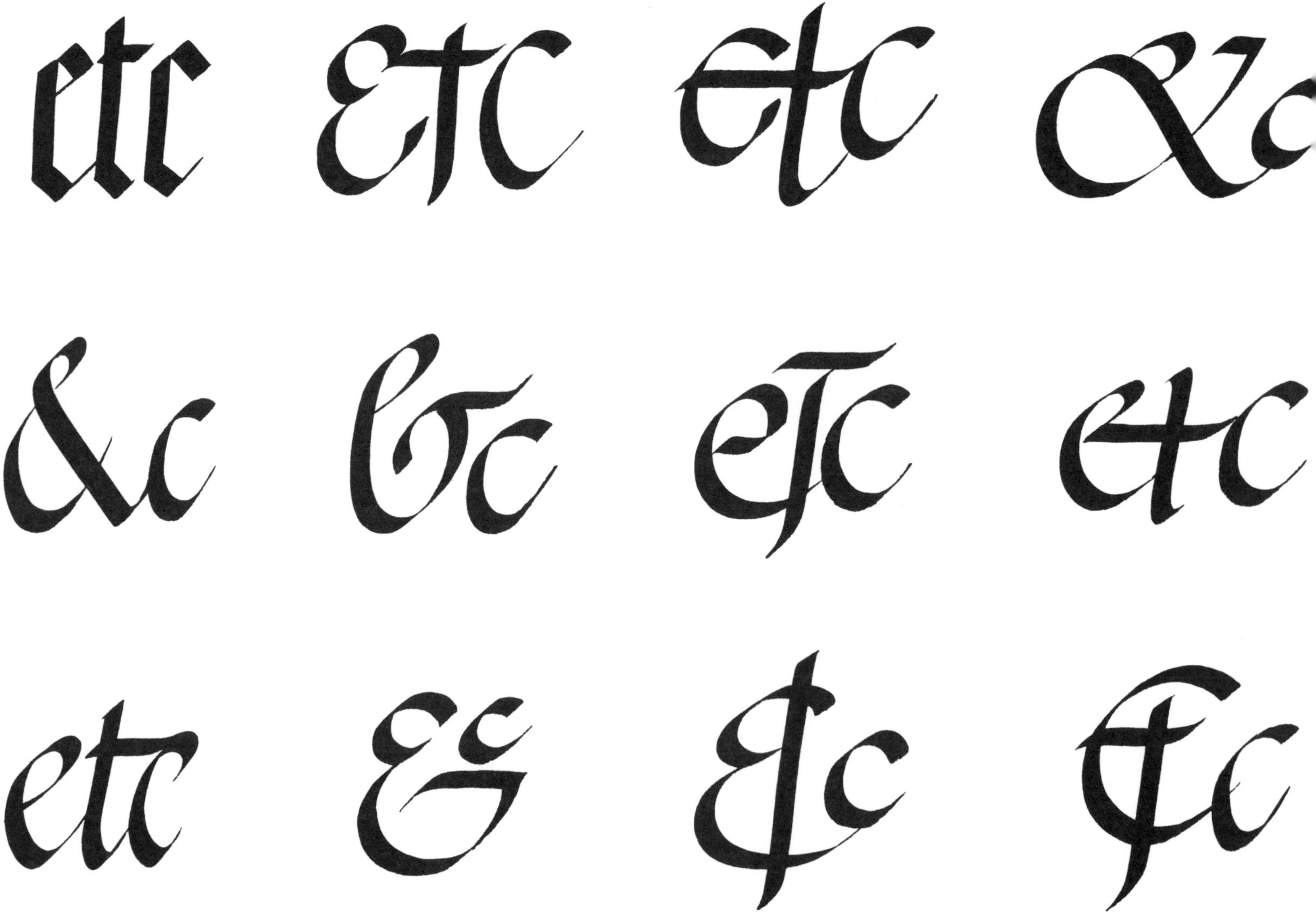

CHAP. I.

*1 Confirming them in hope of the increaſe of God's graces,
5 he exhorteth them by faith and good works, to make
their calling ſure: 16 warneth them to be conſtant in
the faith of Chriſt, &c.*

Bank's Bible 1793

In both these Georgian printed examples we find an
ampersand followed immediately by a lower-case 'c' - a
rather more elegant partnership than our modern etc'.

CARYS
ACTUAL SURVEY
OF THE
COUNTRY
FIFTEEN MILES
ROUND
LONDON.
On a Scale of one Inch to a Mile.
WHEREIN
The Roads, Rivers, Woods and Commons;
AS WELL AS
Every Market Town, Village &c.
ARE DISTINGUISHED:
And every Seat shewn with the Name of the
POSSESSOR.
Preceded by a General Map of the whole.
To which is added,
An Index of all the Names contained in the
PLATES.

LONDON:
Printed for J. CARY, Engraver, Map & Print-ſeller. Nº 181, Strand.
Published as the Act directs, July 1ſt 1817.

Cary's Survey 1817

> Memorand the first day of February in the third yeard of
> the Reigne of o Soueraigne Lord and Lady William & Mary King &
> Queene of England Scottland france & Ireland &c Annoq
> dom 1691 John Blomfeild of Bildston in the sayd County
> fond Coppyhold Tenn of the sayd Mann did Surrender into

> make Him your All in All, and then you will
> want MEANS less, because you TRUST more to
> the God of all means. Exalt & Glorify Him by living
> upon Him, for all things live upon Him. — For
> saving Knowledge He is your Prophet; by whose Life
> & Death alone you can be pardoned & justified at
> the Bar of Iustice. And live upon Him as your King
> to rule in & over you. And then, Thirdly, your

Two examples of everyday scrawl.
The top one is from a vigorously written 'Memorandum' of 1691. Ampersands can be seen towards the ends of lines two and three. The splodgy quality of the writing could be an indication of the writer's ineptitude as a quill cutter.

The lower, more elegant piece is part of an eighteenth-century letter obviously penned by someone of extreme piety with a love of ampersands - there are four in this short section. The finer script suggests that it may have been written with a metal nib.

Apart from personal satisfaction, those who engage in calligraphy will need to become lost in their own concentration for you cannot write well if you or your hand are tense'. Calligraphy then, as some people have discovered, has a great potential as a therapeutic device in a world crowded with other tensions. Writing, & that metaphysical contact between the mind, pen & paper, should, above all, be a matter of pleasure & serenity.

John Vince, author of *Calligraphy / Creating Pictures* uses this very legible hand-written script for the entire text of his book. He makes ample use of his own distinctive ampersand. There are three in the last two lines of this paragraph. Many people, of course, use some sort of cursive italic as their everyday handwriting.

Graphology

The slightly dubious science of graphology does have its highly respectable side. The ability of expert witnesses to identify unconscious traits in samples of handwriting has no doubt been significant in many a court case. Skilled graphologists have been able to see through attempts to disguise handwriting in forgery cases, and have made connections or established authorship by careful analysis of anonymous specimens.

It is also claimed that personal tricks of writing style actually betray hidden aspects of character. This risky procedure, I'm told, is used by employers or their agents when selecting people for key positions. I wonder what effect the pursuit of calligraphic models might have on our chances of landing the right job. The study of handwriting for clues to character presumably requires that the writing is free and uninhibited by formal constraints.

The ways in which people sign their own names is sometimes a give-away when conjuring up personalities. Some signatures, however, are so cryptic they tell us practically nothing: alas, it is usually all that is left after a computer has ironed out any interesting wrinkles there may have been in the original text. The rot really set in with the invention of the typewriter. Graphology was around long before that, of course, and it is even said to have been used by Aristotle, Virgil, Cicero and others.

This is the writing of a strong-willed and forward-looking character - probably quite competitive, but rather impatient - a dynamic personality.

This person is a dreamer - a somewhat frustrated intellectual. However, there are signs of a lively imagination. Innovative, but not good at meeting deadlines.

One very basic example of a graphological principle is the notion that writing is divided into three zones - the upper (which we might call the 'ascenders'), the middle (which we might call the 'x-height'), and the lower (which we might call the 'descenders').
The graphologist, so I understand, thinks in terms of spirit, ambition and imagination in the upper regions; sensuality and materialism in the lower regions; and the middle as the 'here and now' progressing from past to future. It's a neat idea.

An easy-going, sociable individual - quick to make friends. There is nothing devious about this person, but they are perhaps inclined to be impetuous.

Here we have a person of a generous disposition - not a theorist, but an industrious worker with useful practical skills - not suited, however, to high office.

This cheerful and optimistic character is good company, but liable to become confused and indecisive - not the sort of person to be in command of others.

A conscientious team-player - not a leader; useful in a defensive rôle. Too diffident and reflective to spearhead the operation, but patient and reliable.

All the analyses shown here are my own and should not be taken too seriously. I am greatly indebted, however, to the *Handwriting Decoder* published some years ago by Dynamo House in Australia - ISBN 0 949 266 70 1

laudate & super exaltate

Edward Johnston and his associates at the beginning of the 1900s did much to reinstate penscript and the lettering arts. His researches took him back to early medieval monastic examples from which he derived a new systematic approach.

His classic work, *'Writing and Illuminating and Lettering'* first appeared in 1906 in the *'Artistic Crafts Series'* published by John Hogg. Johnston makes passing reference to the 'amperzand' (spelt with a 'z') under the heading 'Monograms & Devices'. He says, "The letter-craftsman will discover many ways of 'playing' with letters, ... and he may take every liberty he chooses in his private pleasure, provided it does not clash with public convenience." (I wonder how he got away with that!)

The book is well illustrated with Johnston's own instructive pieces, already beginning now to look a little quaint, and with time-honoured historical examples where plenty of 'amperzands' may be found. The two shown here are from a 10th.century psalter (above) and a 12th.century breviary (below).

Petri & Pauli

FACTVM EST

uerbum dīu ad ionam filiū amachi.
dicens Surge ce uade in niniuen ci
uitatem magnam. ce prédica in ea.

Another of Johnston's examples, this glorious 'ET' monogram is from a Flemish Latin Bible of 1148. It is unusual for an 'amperzand' to provide the illuminated initial at the beginning of an incipit page. The rounded 'E' is clear enough : the stem of the 'T' is formed by the great fish with Jonah emerging (or being swallowed) above. Johnston was not keen on the text beneath - "not very legible" he says, but it does include a couple of nice chunky little amperzands.

Writing about this fragment from a 13th.century psalter with its curious backward slanting script, Johnston says, "the penmanship exhibits great speed and lightness of hand," - a comment which certainly applies to its delightful line-finishings or fillers.

The four examples below are from the famous 14th.century Luttrell Psalter. These decorative characters may have been added by another illustrator or illuminator. It could be, however, that they provided a little light relief for the scribe himself.

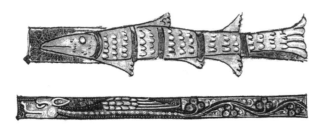

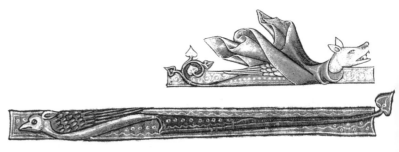

Design gurus* occasionally come over all philosophical when talking about the ampersand. Jessica Helfand describes it as 'a confection to be savored' [sic]. Tom Gleason says 'everyone is always looking for the ideal letterform'. For Michael Hentges 'the ampersand is the preservation of gesture in the printed word' suggesting 'a more immediate presence'. Julie Teninbaum agrees that 'an ampersand is like candy': she sees it 'not as excess, but as a treat: a break from the monotony of type that plays by the rules'. Dmitri Siegel speaks of 'the accumulation over two thousand years of the repressed creativity of scribes and typographers, for whom the ampersand offered the greatest opportunity for flair'. He reckoned that it came to mean more than the word it was designed to represent. In film credits, for example, '&' represents a closer collaboration than 'and'.

It is true that ampersands, these days, are more in evidence in TV titles, book covers and company names. This was not always the case: Eric Gill tried using ampersands throughout the text to the extent that they became obtrusive, and some medieval scribes indulged to excess. It seems clear that they are best used sparingly.

As found on 'Design Observer' website

The title-page from Thomas Tomkins' book of *New Alphabets* with a curious device which could be some kind of ampersand. The happy relationship between 'Copperplate' and 'Engravers' Gothic' has been achieved by the rather extravagant use of flourishes. Published in 1779, it is to be hoped that the youth of the day were suitably 'improved'!

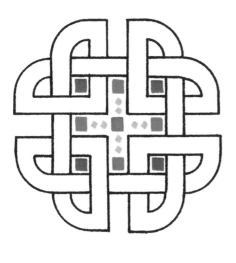

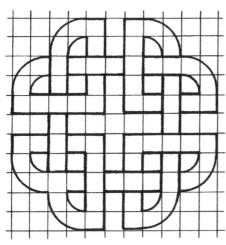

'Celtic' decoration

Some of our greatest treasures, such as the Lindisfarne Gospels or the Book of Kells, inscribed well over a thousand years ago, are enriched with the most intricate decoration. At its most distinctive, this is often in the form of 'knotwork' which is also found carved on ancient standing stones, and in Anglo-Saxon jewellery. The style is loosely referred to as 'Celtic'. Although originally used in conjunction with ancient scripts - uncials, for example, and curious straight line, rather 'Runic' letters, knotwork continues to look quite at home with other not-so-ancient kinds of calligraphy.

Shown here are two very plain versions. The diagrams show how this sort of thing can be drawn, based on a simple squared grid. Draw the grid in pencil which can be erased when the pattern has been inked in. The little coloured 'tesserae' can be quickly added using a broad calligraphic nib.

Creating pictorial textures with typographic
devices was one way of using up the
oddments left over on sheets of transfer
lettering. Now that computer typesetting has
taken over, this pastime may be a little more
difficult.

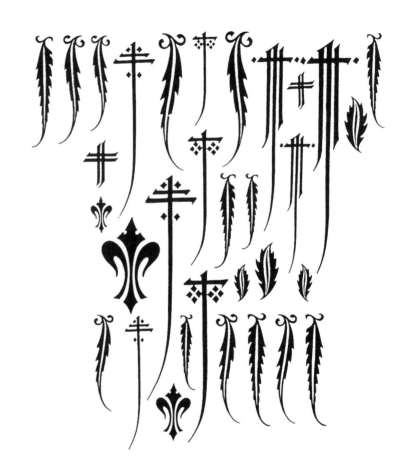

Florets

Chisel-shaped nibs produce distinctive shapes - hence different styles of script. In addition to letter-forms, however, they can be used simply to make patterns, useful as borders or fillers. One such application is the construction of roundels or florets - radiating designs, either in monochrome or in many colours. There is plenty of scope for originality here.

Springing from the same writing implements, these designs have an in-built affinity with penscript, so they are a fitting accompaniment to many a calligraphic inscription when making book covers, cards, posters and so on.

First make a faint pencil 'skeleton' like a darts-board, using compasses and protractor. Then add concentric circles with various repeating penstrokes, turning the paper as you go, and making sure not to smudge what you have just drawn - a useful exercise in pen manipulation.

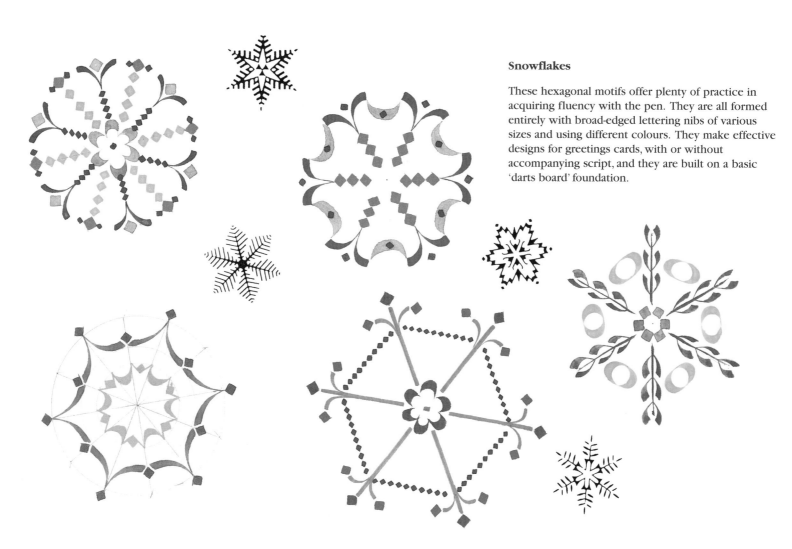

Snowflakes

These hexagonal motifs offer plenty of practice in acquiring fluency with the pen. They are all formed entirely with broad-edged lettering nibs of various sizes and using different colours. They make effective designs for greetings cards, with or without accompanying script, and they are built on a basic 'darts board' foundation.

Transfer Lettering

Printers' fists

Not much in evidence today, these printers' fists still have their uses for emphasis and direction. The earliest examples were probably wood-cuts. Calligraphic script usually looks very much at home with any wood-cut illustration. The examples here, however, have been cast in metal: those at the top, pointing right, are all 19th.century, except for the little solid black one designed by Eric Gill early in the 20th.century. The two pointing left are also 20th.century.

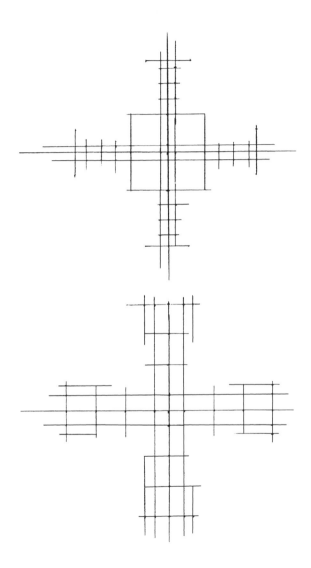

Calligraphic Crosses

The simplest of all 'ampersands' is probably the cross or plus sign. The decorative examples shown here, however, are unlikely to be of much practical use in that respect. They do, nevertheless, serve beautifully as jewel-like ornaments, and since they are produced entirely with the familiar chisel-shaped nib or brush they look very much at home in conjunction with calligraphic script. There are, of course, endless variations on the theme.

Inventing crosses can provide much useful practice in the use of calligraphic nibs and are valuable as first exercises - adjusting angles and judging distances. They could be allowed to evolve as 'doodles', but most scribes, I suspect, will feel more comfortable working within a pencil grid. The larger nib sizes will be more useful as a start and the paper will need to be turned frequently - beware of smudging while the paint is wet.

Two ampersands involving plain crosses

Swedenborg

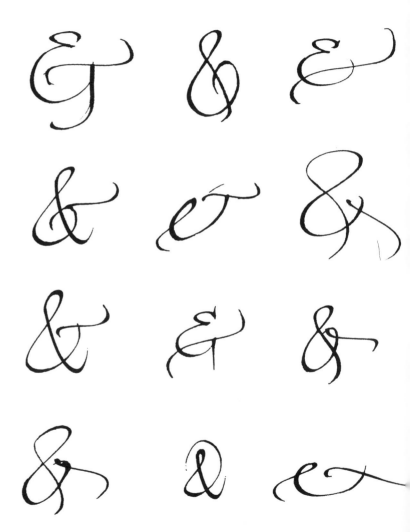

Mary Noble, one of our foremost scribes produced all the examples on these two pages. Having clearly studied historical and typographic examples, she has reinterpreted them with characteristic verve. Unlike typeset versions, no two are alike. Thus recent calligraphy tends towards the visually expressive rather than the more formal work of past ages.

This lively assortment, with its dancing line, looks as though the scribe really enjoyed doing them. It is perhaps not surprising that Gothic letter forms are not much in evidence, but these flowing examples will surely inspire a more daring use of the pen.

I am grateful for the privilege of including them here.

Calligraphic Expressionism

It doesn't actually say anything at all - so far as I know.

Cartouches, Rules & Ornaments

Cartouches are not hard to find: antique maps are a
rich source of extremely ornate examples. They can
also be 'borrowed' from old books and documents.
Most of these are engravings. Another approach, of
course, is to draw them calligraphically using broad
script nibs of various sizes. This usually ensures that
there is some affinity between the frame and the
inscription within. The technique involves much
adjusting of angles and rotation of paper.

··· Christus Dominus ···

Bees use the sun to find the nectar. Even when the sky is cloudy the sun is always there. Their eyes are made so that they can see it. God is our sun. His love and wisdom are always there however clouded our life may seem.

BEE GUIDED BY HIM

Use of different implements

Pictograms

It seems to be generally agreed that, thousands of years ago, writing of some sort probably began with pictograms - pictures of things reduced to as few lines as possible. The broad lettering nibs that most of us use today, however, scarcely lend themselves to picture making, but our more light-hearted inscriptions can sometimes be enlivened with the addition of simplified 'cartoons' using the same kind of pen as for the text so that the whole thing looks 'all of a piece'. The trick is to think of the pictogram as a calligraphic device rather than an illustration. This means cutting down the drawing drastically, leaving a lot to the imagination. Such images are seldom as easy as they may look.

A more elaborate example: this has been drawn
entirely with broad-edged nibs in three or four sizes.
The design is freely based on a piece of antique Chinese
lacquerwork. A classical Oriental calligrapher would,
no doubt, use a brush to greater effect.

In this water clear as air, lurks a lobster

c d e a
g j n

The Owl and the Pussy Cat
The Owl and the Pussy Cat went to sea in a beautiful pea green boat. They took some honey,

you are old Father William, the young man said, and your hair has become very white, and yet you incessantly stand on your head

Pentagon

VERSE

Cartouche

DANIEL

f

This is a set of information. Be careful not to run out of space, you can get in quite a lot of information. Start in the middle in case you run out of space. You can get in quite a lot of information. Start in the middle in case you run out of space. Circles as you will see from the diagram alongside. It is a continuation of staggered semi-circles as you will see a not a proper spiral.

ffffff

Two Centres

1
2

Do you think at your age that is right

gh
e
Pen&Ink
Pen&Ink
Pen&Ink
Pen&Ink
&

Gothic

These Victorian and Edwardian examples are taken from old legal assurance documents. They display that distinctively cursive style of handwriting which has become known as Copperplate. Seldom seen in business today, it seems that many of our great-grandfathers were adept in this elegant hand. As the name implies, it originated as an engraved letter-form, the swelling thickness of the stroke springing from the depth of the graver in metal. For everyday correspondence in ink, however, the writer would use some form of pliant and pointed implement.

Though clearly disciplined, we can detect subtle differences between one scribe and another. The two lower examples give us the chance to compare the same wording from two different writers with a five-year interval between. The finer line of the lowermost version, very noticeable in the capital 'B', could possibly denote the arrival of the steel pen nib. The Birmingham nib business was very well established by this time.

The London & Lancashire Life Assurance Company.

1883

An engraved title from the Girls' Own Annual 1903

T. M. the King & Queen from the painting by Alyn Williams & Hal Hurst.

Messrs H. & C. Briggs

1903

Messrs H. & C. Briggs

1908

1867

1896

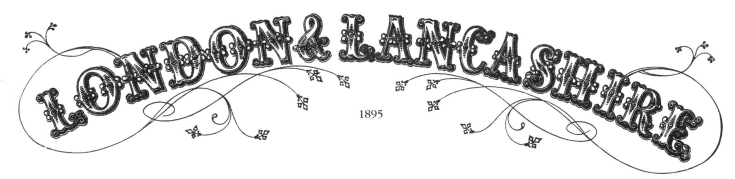

1895

𝕳are & Co., 𝕷td., 𝕭ride 𝕮ourt, 𝕱leet 𝕾treet
𝕻hoto=𝕰ngravers, etc.

SEND ONE SHILLING FOR SAMPLE BOOK

Trade has promoted some of the worst and some of the very best in typographic and calligraphic design. In all these examples the on-going influence of Gothic penscript is still clearly in evidence.

On the left are two examples from the 19th century. The meticulous label above was in use not long ago in the middle of the 20th century.

Headings from Victorian times show that engraving on metal had reached a high degree of craftsmanship, wonderfully exploited here with plenty of elaborate ornament. Since then things seem to have been getting plainer over the years, although the gothic style persists even today in some quarters where old-established reliability is the watchword. The 'gothic' ampersand in the last of these examples is not much different from that in the first.

Meanwhile a calligraphic style again makes its appearance, shown here in the bold penscript of the Pears' advertisement from 1925. This clearly shows the influence of Edward Johnston and his associates - I doubt that it is by the great man himself.

1915

1925

1929

1966

ART & GENERAL INS

From an insurance policy 1939

Despite its easy-going ampersand, this
heading - clearly hand-drawn - shows scant
regard for the classical proportions of
'Monumental Roman Capitals' from which, I
suppose, it was meant to be derived.

Two curious devices fom The Monotype Corporation, mid 20th century

Over a hundred years ago, in 1905, A A Turbayne of the Carlton Studio in London produced a truly monumental work *Monograms & Ciphers* in which he and his apprentices assembled many hundreds of designs. These were all hand-drawn, of course, and were intended for engraving on metal. We now loosely refer to such designs as 'monograms'. Turbayne insists, however, that a *monogram* is a device where two or more letters actually *combine* so that part of one letter also forms part of another - inseparably: all the rest are *ciphers*. These days we have little time for such pedantry. Nearly all the lettering in Turbayne's remarkable book is 'drawn' rather than 'pen-written'. The ampersand features in lots of these examples, and can fairly easily be translated into calligraphic terms.

MONOGRAMS & · CIPHERS

DESIGNED · AND · DRAWN · BY
A · A · TURBAYNE
AND
OTHER · MEMBERS · OF · THE
· CARLTON ·
STUDIO

LONDON
THE · CAXTON · PUBLISHING · CO
MDCCCCV

Two more not very successful attempts at transposing a drawn cipher into a pen-written device.

Drawn lettering, as distinct from penscript, is more labour-intensive, usually requiring the careful drawing of outlines and infilling. At the same time, however, there is greater freedom to elaborate: fancy serifs and swelled versal-like letterforms are all in order - no holds barred. The tendency is to *embellish*, sometimes even harking back to 'Celtic' knotwork.

Pen lettering, on the other hand, tends to *simplify* since the broad nib imposes its own restraints: the thicks and thins inevitably arising from pen angles.

Either way, devices of this kind need careful planning with plenty of experimental tracing paper to hand.

The three examples below all incorporate an ampersand with two attachments forming '& Co'.

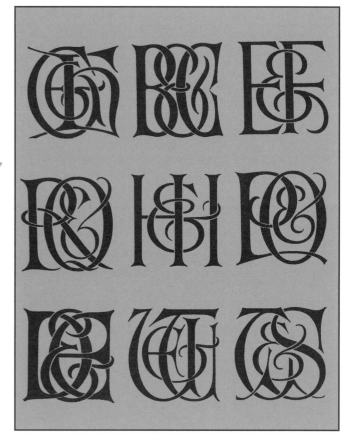

Another selection of Turbayne's ciphers. Not always easy to *de*cipher, all these involve an ampersand as the connecting link between two letters.

Much fine calligraphy is still inspired by religious ideas, even in this 21st.century. The church has not entirely lost its time-honoured rôle as patron of the arts, commissioning these days some beautifully inscribed texts and memorials, but very few complete gospels - there is, after all, no need for them now. This traditional function of the church can be traced back almost to its very beginnings when book production was for centuries a monastic monopoly. Despite some pretty primitive working conditions, they produced works of amazing beauty and incredible craftsmanship. On title pages they might happily muddle up the letters a bit for the sake of the visual effect.

This is what Turbayne has done here with his *'Sacred Devices'* of 1906. The statements are short, and the reader might anyway be expected to know in advance what they say.

A pen-written interpretation

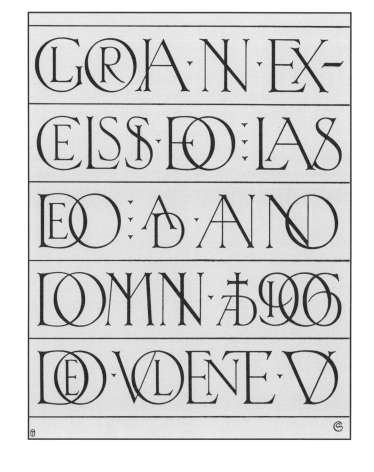

Many of us, I suppose, first learned the alphabet at an early age by chanting from beginning to end, finishing perhaps with a triumphant "and 'and' by itself": hence and-per-se or *ampersand*. The French *esperluette* flows maybe more easily from the tongue. In Scotland, I believe, it is known as an *epershand*. The ampersand has also been referred to as "a break from the monotony of type that plays by the rules, a creative doodle amongst measured letterforms."
(Julie Teninbaum). Ampersands are recognised in various countries, regardless of language differences: they may thus be said to be almost international. They are the links in an alphabetical chain: what they denote is often a 'partnership', not an 'accumulation', in situations where an ordinary plus sign + simply would not do.

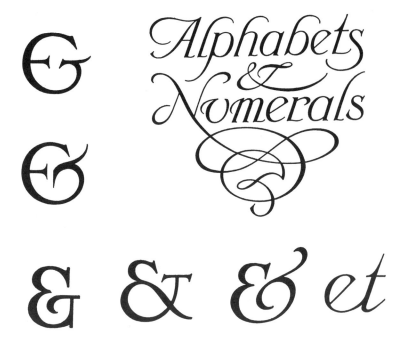

Some more examples from Turbayne's *Monograms & Ciphers* of 1905. None of these is pen-written: they are all 'drawn' letters, including the highly flourished 'N'.

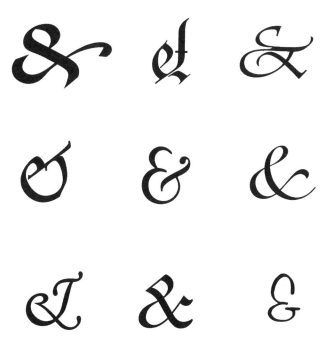

Here and overleaf we have a selection of typeset ampersands ranging from the rather brutal ultra bold modern examples to the more classical italic styles.

Calligraphic versions tend to be more in evidence among the lightweight specimens whose origins may be traced back to the 16th & 17th centuries.

Most of these can, no doubt, be encountered among the so-called 'fonts' available on a computer. The word derives from 'fount' or 'found', because in the days of metal type-setting that was where the letters came from - a type-foundry. A fount would then have comprised about 150 'sorts' - letters, spaces, symbols etc. - supplied in quantities more or less in proportion to their utility.

Typeset letter forms usually look rather mechanical and intrusive when used in company with calligraphic work, but they can sometimes be adapted and embellished to advantage.

Outlines and shadow-lines

These typeset examples with their three-dimensional overtones make distinctive statements which, in the right context, can be effective.

The animated version with its head and tail reminds us of medieval marginal grotesques, but it is a feeble imitation.

A simple outline can impart elegance to a letter-form, and all these ampersands present opportunities for coloured infilling: some suggest moulded or incised forms.

Weight problems

The printed or written letter can whisper, or it can shout. Usually, in polite conversation it should do neither, but there are occasions when extremes will serve to make a point more dramatically.

New directions

These seem to be in process of evolving into something else.
The original *'et'* can still be found, but it is now stretched into some
interesting new shapes, from which the flowing lines of earlier
centuries have all but disappeared.

Stencils

These chunky functional examples, derived from the practicalities
of the tea chest and the packing station, have now come to
represent almost anything remotely commercial.

And these might have been squeezed out of a toothpaste tube.

From the sublime to the ridiculous

These ampersands, despite their casual quirky appearance, are all taken from computer typefaces, characteristic, no doubt, of the decadent age in which we live.

The writing masters and type founders of times gone by will be turning in their graves on seeing the depths to which we have sunk.

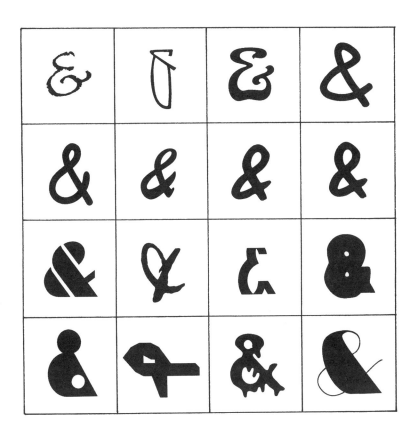

The typographer's stock in trade

Press-button technology means that the typographer is spoilt for choice. Freed from traditional constraints, all sorts of strange anomalies can occur - and often do. The same 'fonts' sometimes appear under different names with perhaps only the ampersand redesigned for legal reasons. We see here a selection of type-faces - sans serif on the left, serifed on the right, roughly arranged by weight. Each of these ampersands is subtly different from all the others.

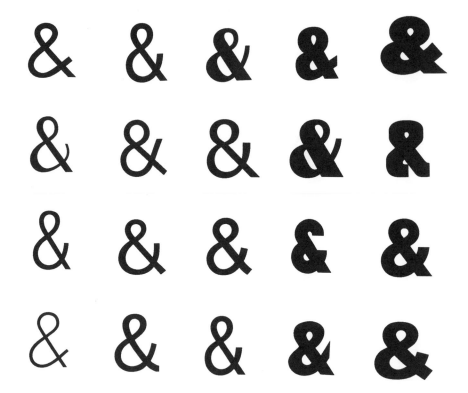

'Playbill' - an interesting
attempt to achieve
boldness with clarity in a
tight place.

A computerised version
with a distinctly calligraphic
quality, and just the merest
suggestion of serifs.

A Calligraphy of Types or Types of Calligraphy?

Hammering away at our computers, few of us ever give heed to the fact that every letter, if only we could trace its ancestry back far enough, would turn out to have been drawn or written by someone. Somewhere along the line, type matter had to be designed and we find that many of our most skilful type designers are - or were - great calligraphers. The quill continues to haunt the digital devilry of our time. This is mostly evident in some of the so-called 'italic' faces with their distinctive slant and drive. The serifed Roman faces still tend, generally speaking, to reflect the thick/thin characteristics of the broad-edged pen.

In the next few pages I have gathered together some examples of those founts or 'fonts' that best reveal their calligraphic origins. In Germany, type styles often refined and perpetuated their 'Gothic' roots, whilst here in Britain 'Old English' came to be associated with the antiques business, old-world charm and reliability. In Victorian England, children with their newly invented steel nibs were bullied into the mysteries of 'Copperplate' handwriting, so, as adults they penned their formal invitations and legal documents using precisely that. Then the education of children changed of course, and type founders quickly filled the gap with founts such as 'Palace Script', still popular today. Such niceties are of little use when naming country railway stations: from your first-class compartment, rushing past at speed, you would need a kind of print whose message might be taken in at a glance – hence the arrival of a new breed of no-nonsense functional sans-serif letters evident on main lines, and notably on the London Underground.

eva & zeno polycarp
quintilian alexius

American
Uncial Titling

American
Uncial Titling

abcdefghijklmnopqrstuvwxyzåő
úchfftt1234567890

Unziale

Anything less 'American' than uncials is hard to imagine, but all these examples clearly derive from that ancient script, and 'American Uncial Titling' most obviously so.

Its rather clumsy relation 'Unziale' has its uses where a compact and chunky look may be needed, despite some quirky numbers. 'Libra' is more immediately legible and has a distinctive weight of its own.

For a free-ranging uncial character, 'Andromaque' offers continuous text for the light of heart.

vorueber! ach, vorueber!
geh, wilder knochenmann!
Ich bin noch jung! geh, lieber!
und ruehre mich nicht an.

gib deine hand, du schoen und zart gebild!
bin freund und komme nicht zu strafen.
sei gutes muts! ich bin nicht wild,
sollst sanft in meinen armen schlafen!

Andromaque

the quick brown fox
over the lazy dog

Libra

ABCDEFGHIJKLMNOPQ
abcdefghijklmnopqrstuvwxyz &

Codex

ABCDEF
GHIJKL
MNOPQ
RSTUVW
XY&Z

Molé Foliate

I don't know quite what to make of 'Codex'. It does have calligraphic overtones and the capitals seem to owe something to uncials, but we are approaching the 'Roman' rather than the 'Celtic' here. The other four examples are unashamedly regimented and Roman, owing more to print than penmanship, although 'Decorata' looks as though it might be achieved by writing, and 'Egmont Inline' is reminiscent of versals.

SUPERBE

Cristal

ABCDE

Egmont Inline Titling

GENESIS

Decorata

Die Kunst ist ein ernsthaftes Geschäft, am ernsthaftesten,

Die Klugheit ist zwar sehr geeignet, zu erhalten was man besitzt, aber allein die Kühnheit läßt gewinnen.   Friedrich der Große

Claudius

ABCDEFGHIJKLMNOPQ RSTUVWXYZ   AÖÜ abcdefghijklmnopqrstuvwxyz &

Trump Deutsch

I wonder what Gutenberg might have thought about this lot. Their obvious scriptural derivation still serves to bring the Middle Ages into current usage, and the jobbing calligrapher is all the richer for it. I am intrigued to see, however, what happens when someone takes what is essentially an upright, respectable, well-regimented style and tries to ginger it up a bit. The swash characters from 'Gilgengart' overleaf – if so they be – are a springboard for the more abandoned lettering so much in favour today.

Gilgengart · ABCDEF
GHIJKLMNOPQ
RSTUVWXYZ abc
defghijklmnopqrstuvwxyz

ABCDEFGHI
JKLMNOPQR

often to be working, and both should be gentlemen, in
the best sense. As it is, we make both ungentle, the one
envying, the other despising his brother; and society
is made up of morbid thinkers and miserable workers.

Manual of modern advertising
Brunswick Map Printers

Palatino

The basic character in a type design is determined by the uniform design characteristics of all letters in the alphabet.

Galliard

It is in their italic versions that type-faces usually best reveal their calligraphic origins. One of the more recent of these is 'Palatino' – an elegant face, very legible, preserving nuances of weight which would be difficult to sustain manually. The others on this page, by comparison, are just a shade heavy-handed, except, maybe, for 'Delphin' – this curious style is particularly notable for its verticality.

abcdefghijklmnopqrstuvwxyzæœfiflffiffflff

Spectrum

abcddefgghijklmnopqrstuvwxyz   äöü chckß

Delphin

abcdefghijklmnopqrstuvwxyz

Hyperion

I am not entirely convinced that these eccentricities could be achieved with a pen, but they do look as though they may have started life that way. Individual letters – especially the capitals – are interesting enough in themselves, though I suspect they may not always be totally at ease with their lower-case bedfellows. A little of this sort of thing goes a long way.

les feuilles éparpillées 1234567890
ABCDEFGHIJKLMNOPQR

Auriol

AABBCDDEEFEGHIJ
OPQRRSSTTUVWX

abcdefghijklmnopqrstuvwxyz

Amalthea

Fashions change, and each
tastes. That is to say, of the
WHICH THE ARTIST CAN

Matura

HIJKLMNOPQRST
abcdefghijklmnopqrstuvwxyz
1234567890

Legend

92

Some more bits and pieces from the ragbag.

℮ & & & &

ßatz& & &

ÆŒ

& 𝕭𝖆𝖉𝖒𝖆𝖓 ℐ A B C

.,:;-!?.'()[]*†‹›»«„"/£$ Q ALPHABET

(.,-;:!i?¿—) .,:;-!?"(*†‡§[£$ƒ— £ QRS

'!?..-;:,$ ⁊]+−=/$£†*&§

POSTSCRIPT

Since the first tentative scratchings on cave walls, calligraphy has undergone many changes and has now reached the stage where, with the aid of a computer and a screen, letters can be contorted before our very eyes at the touch of a keyboard. Over the centuries techniques and purposes have moved with the times, and what I would call the 'spirit' of writing has changed accordingly. Why do people still engage in such an exacting pursuit when there are so many quicker ways of doing it?

My wife wins more prizes for her home-made marmalade when I write the labels, but there is more to it than that - much more! When the ancient Sumerians first started prodding messages into their little slabs of clay, they were probably more concerned with their accounts than with their calligraphy - they were not renowned for their jam making. The Egyptians, painting pictograms on the walls of tombs, or writing with reed-pens on papyrus, may have taken the utmost care, but they were just as interested in recording their military exploits as they were in their penmanship. The Romans, famous for their monumental inscriptions, when they weren't chipping away at triumphal arches, they were maybe jotting down notes on slivers of wood, or issuing imperial orders on papyrus scrolls. Then came the monks with quill and parchment, diligently copying lengthy works of scholarship and devotion, often with the most meticulous and magical illumination. We still marvel at their craftsmanship but their prime motive, of course, was to celebrate, preserve and perpetuate the Word of God. They may have had their league tables, I suppose, with each scriptorium competing for the coveted 'Golden Quill Award' or the 'Manuscript of the Year', but somehow I doubt it: there were more important issues at stake.

Johannes Gutenberg properly upset the age-old apple-cart of alphabets when he finally came up with moveable type. He has a lot to answer f However, not to be out-manoeuvred, the scribes successfully exploited growing demand for one-off documents - agreements, contracts, treatie: etc. The Renaissance writing masters soon discovered a market for littl handbooks offering guidance to the uninitiated in the form of amazing exemplars, ostensibly for education but, I suspect, as a means of flaunti their own considerable calligraphic skills. Then, almost last among the professionals, came the scriveners, laborious exponents of Victorian copperplate, with steel nibs to their pens, inscribing legal documents.

They all had their reasons, many of which have now been lost with the advent of new technology. Even letter-writing is in danger of becoming lost art and the structures of language itself, always volatile, seem to be changing more rapidly than ever. Inevitably the calligrapher seeks motivation elsewhere. Visual effects are taking over where legibility us to be pre-eminent. Ideally, how a piece looks and what it is supposed t be saying should be symbiotic - mutually supportive, I would have thought: but letter-forms these days often mutate in unexpected ways. The 'scritchy-scratchy' approach, for example, appears to be a fashionab sign-of-the-times: apparent spontaneity has become a virtue; a piece ma look as though it has been dashed off in a creative frenzy when, in fact is the result of prolonged analysis. I was once showing my students some acclaimed avant-garde examples when one of them cried out, "Bu I've only now thrown away something just like that!" Whereas texture might once have been superficial - not part of the substance of the wo - it now sometimes becomes an end in itself with the letters hard to fin ligraphy has overflowed its traditional boundaries, and I am at pains to nt out to my people that they are now perfectly entitled to write *as y wish*. In reply to the question "How does this go?" I may ddeningly say "Well, how do you want it to go?"

enever a body of 'experts' sets itself apart as a society or association guild or something of that sort, it usually starts to discriminate ween those who are fit to join, and those who are not, and so claims rôle of arbiter in the bid for 'recognition'. This has happened with okery, needlework, flower-arranging, sugarcraft, gardening and heaven ows what else: calligraphy has certainly succumbed to this insidious laise. It is a sad thing because it inevitably turns an art form into a mpetitive sport. What is essentially a means of communication comes instead an obstacle race. Calligraphy is a means of expressing versity: creative people do not need to be graded like eggs. emember one of my own teachers would often greet some new ation with the wise remark, "It's very clever, but is it art?"

lligraphy has much to offer as a form of therapy. I have had a few abled students, and even those with obstinate fingers have found tering useful once we found an appropriate style. They might not ever n any prizes, but that is not the point. The pursuit of letters can be nderfully diverting if you don't take them too seriously. Many of those o come to my classes are escaping from the pressures of their rking week and they simply enjoy figuring out calligraphic puzzles. the process, they usually acquire a basic skill that just 'comes in handy' announcement for the notice-board - a birthday card - some place ds for a party - nothing too sophisticated. We also enjoy each other's mpany - calligraphers are *always* the most charming of people!

But the dizzy heights of the professional super-scribe are probably attained only by those who may not have much else to do: they are the ones who tour the world exhibiting their work, writing books, and commanding high prices. Their mission in life is to be an inspiration to the rest of us, but we do try not to be intimidated by them: after all, they are a minority, and they are seldom as infallible as they seem.

I once had a very interesting discussion with a friendly graphologist: her job was to study specimens of normal handwriting, comparing details and discerning character from personal idiosyncrasies in the script. Her work was of use to the police when examining written evidence. My friend agreed that being exposed to formal calligraphy could inhibit individual styles of writing, and thus make her work less reliable - advocates of 'Italic' handwriting would no doubt be particularly prone to such an influence.

Most primary schools have a doctrinaire approach to the teaching of handwriting to children which presumably has some effect on their mature style later on, but this is one of those subjects which, with reliance now-a-days on the computer, tends, alas, to go by the board. It would be a pity if we were to so channel teaching methods as to iron out all the interesting wrinkles. In my experience, most calligraphers also have an everyday scrawl like anyone else.

The history of letters is pursued these days more assiduously than ever before. With the help of a scholarly élite we now have access to an understanding of old manuscripts denied to earlier scribes who may never have reviewed their own work, or anyone else's, in its historical context. We inherit a richly varied array of antiquarian material which could so easily have been lost if it were not for the work of these learned masterminds. The recent salvation of the Macclesfield Psalter is but one prime example. It is difficult to be precise about the ultimate purpose of all this erudition: it has little practical application that I can see, but without it civilisation would be greatly impoverished.

Our perception of a text is largely pre-conditioned. We each bring to bear an association of ideas which is probably not quite the same as anyone else's. There are, however, common connections: faced with a Gothic script, many people could assume that it may have something to do with a church or an antiques business: a sparse functional Sans-Serif, on the other hand, could suggest a work about electronics: an Italic might reflect something more lyrical. In my own case, after a long time snooping about looking at other people's work, the *style* is what now prompts my reaction, not the content. I come away with a clear impression of the writing, but remember absolutely nothing about what it actually *said*. One of my students, who happens to be an accomplished author, finds this quite infuriating. It is, I suggest, the subtle manipulation of these associations that makes the whole business so interesting. Visual style speaks more immediately than syntax, but it is not nearly so articulate. It is helpful to have a good battery of styles in one's armoury, and this is where a little learning does not come amiss.

We cherish the work of previous generations, treasures from times long gone, and so we should because they are the windows into another world. I wonder whether in centuries to come the alphabetical boffins will peer back from cyberspace and look at *our* work and think 'how quaint'. Will our efforts go down in history; will they last; does it matter if they don't? I am not so sure: for all its incredible cleverness, much of our present output lacks something vital. Maybe it has lost an underlying sense of purpose: it is no longer *'necessary'*. Some of it will certainly survive, especially that which is enshrined within the covers of a book protected from the viruses of time. Much of the rest, though highly entertaining while it lasts, is ephemeral, to be hung on a wall for a while and then forgotten.

G. Roland Smith 2008